COLOURING
DELIGHTS

with poetic insight

Colouring, Poems, Join the Dots

By
Ruth Irwin

PLEASE NOTE: IDENTICAL DRAWINGS ARE USED IN TWO COLOURING BOOKS BY RUTH IRWIN: "COLOURING FUN FOR EVERYONE" AND "COLOURING DELIGHTS WITH POETIC INSIGHT."

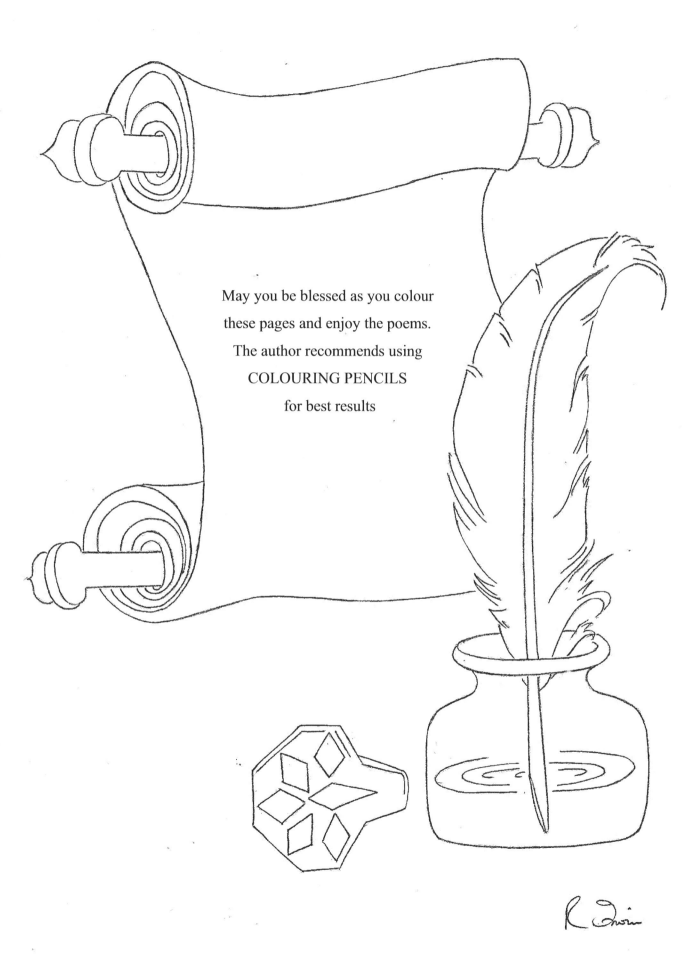

May you be blessed as you colour
these pages and enjoy the poems.
The author recommends using
COLOURING PENCILS
for best results

CONTENTS

List of Poems with DRAWINGS to colour

Followed by JOIN-THE-DOTS pages

Please see end pages for further information about the Author

AMAZING COMPLEXITIES

I am (you are) a spiritual being, capabilities untold
Mysteries you can unravel as the path of life unfolds.
In an earthen vessel made of clay, a spirit person lives;
In human form a living soul, that sees, moves and gives.

Within this spirit person, (golden bowl) there is a void, a space;
A deep longing for the Master's love that nothing can replace.
A silver cord of life attaches spirit being to God;
In Christ we live, move, and have our being,
though all this seems quite odd.

We're far too complicated for anyone to fathom,
Our spirit, body and soul converge in particles of light and atoms.
Countless cells construct our bodies, un-imaginable is the feat,
Yet the God of all creations love, was demonstrated in defeat.

We can compare to specks of dust, viewed from His great perspective.
Yet powered by His Grace and Love, we live unexplainably interactive,
A mellow form, which glows and knows, that moves, walks and speaks.
A heavenly scent was given us, which now lost in sin; just reeks.

In between the realms of life, a natural man, yet spiritual,
Divine health, provision, providence flow from His throne,
to every intellectual.

Praise and thanks activates the power of His Name,
He bore our sins upon the cross, when He languished there in shame.
Alive now forevermore He lives and reigns in Glory,
Eternal life we can enjoy, choose Life, live in His story.

ACORN POTENTIAL

Inside a tiny acorn, lying dormant in the ground;
There is powerful potential, that somehow does astound.
In solitude it sleeps, deep within the cold, dark earth;
Pressured, squeezed, uncomfortable, until there is new birth.

Cotyledons full of strength, put forth a tiny root.
As upwards, creeping onwards; a little stem does shoot.
Growing towards the sunlight, it emerges in the spring,
While its roots dig deeper, downwards; nourishment to bring.

This tiny little sapling, turns from plant, into a towering tree,
Gigantic, strong and powerful; for all the world to see.
Under its shady leaves and branches, children love to play;
And if you listen carefully, you may hear the acorn say:

"When pressured with life's problems, do not despair, there's hope;
Progression is an onward quest, with ever expanding scope.
You are strong, with great potential, mighty as can be,
Don't be afraid, be bold; press on, un-pack it just like me."

AN ODE TO ODI

A soft shiny coat, beautiful and dark,
Tiny pattering feet that love walks in the park.
Adorable brown eyes, so full of expression,
Meekness and kindness, all brimming in session.

Very smart, very elegant; a haircut, a new look.
He's so loving and special; from a fairy tale book.
A much-loved character this welcome guest,
He has touched our hearts; we are very blessed.

There's always some food in his own special plate,
'Grace' must be said, before he can eat.
He gazes at me, puts his paw on my hand,
I now say the grace, he then waits for command.

He's an obedient dog in his own special way;
Very charming, affectionate, he knows he can stay.
Comfortably sits on the sofa, or just on our laps;
Watches television, or has a short nap.

He visits us very often, this dear loving friend,
He has two missing toes; on a foot, that did mend.
A handsome Cocker spaniel, a very special dog;
He enjoys the open countryside;
always happy on a jog.

ANTS

Ants are tiny insects, of the family 'Formicidae'.
They cleverly form colonies, in sophisticated ways.
Twelve thousand different species, all around the world;
A hundred trillion ants on earth, as statistics are unfurled.

These fascinating creatures, when foraging for food,
Leave a specific chemical signal, a 'pheromone trail', prelude.
Pristomyrmex pungens, do not construct a nest,
Yet they set up a kingdom, without queen or male; a quest!

There are many topical ant species:
'Pharaohs ants' and 'Rogers ghost';
These survive in warmth, in winter months,
In the houses of their hosts.

Ants are all eusocial, highest level of organisation,
Complexity in simplicity, they're found in every nation.
Ants don't have ears; and yet they hear;
By feeling vibrations in the ground.
Through their feet so sensitive, they can decipher sound.

Ants don't have lungs; yet they breathe,
Through pores in all their bodies.
Queens, males, workers and soldier ants, live together in hierarchies.
Some ants bite, others many sting, some instead spray formic acid,
Clumped together, known as rafts,
Resilient; survive floods and rapids.

Ants have many colonies, under wood piles, or in dead trees,
In the ground or above the ground, they always seem at ease.
Extremely smart and organised, these are a clever lot,
Carpenter, Fire, and Pavement ants, Black garden ants, all sorts!
Learn diligence from these creatures,
As they work, and store their food,
Teamwork in perfect harmony, persistence is always good.

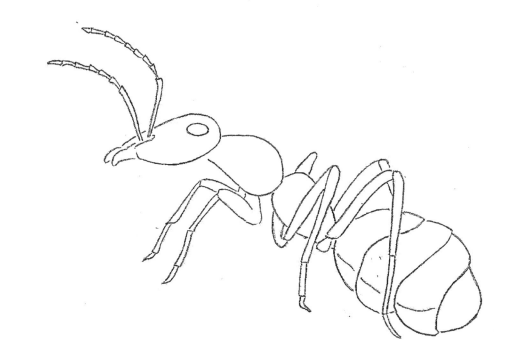
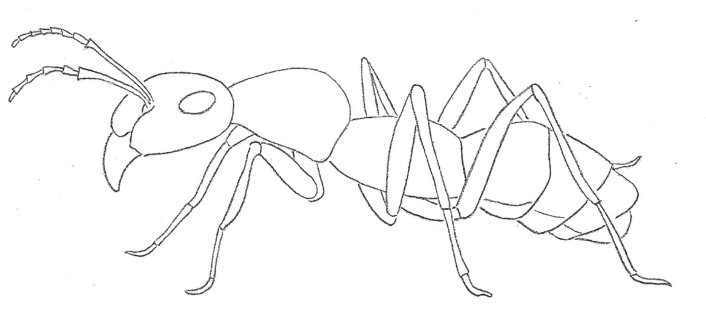

AT BRANDE

The Danish town of Brande, Three 'D' paintings in the square,
Viewed through telescope or camera lens; depict images in the air.
This beautiful place is famous, for it's fantastic works of art;
Where the walls of shops are painted, along the central mart:

A dancing girl and butterflies! An old lady at a window,
Alice in wonderland, so tall! Balloons and a giant rainbow.
Fierce looking Vikings, in an ancient ship,
A drowning girl, ghost in a boat, what an entertaining trip.

In a restaurant named "NOA", we had Mexican cuisine,
Delicious food with spices, to the senses that appeal.
The local school looked elegant, a building with a large clock.

A Quirky cottage with the Roses, Lises' home around the block.
The pristine church yard and building, like a fortress, looming tall,
Lise sat upon the bench outside, while I in awe admired all.

The town held many memories, for my dearest, kindest friend,
We treasured every moment, as we walked around each bend.
Many photographs were taken, precious memories to keep,
To cheer me up on rainy days, before I go to sleep.

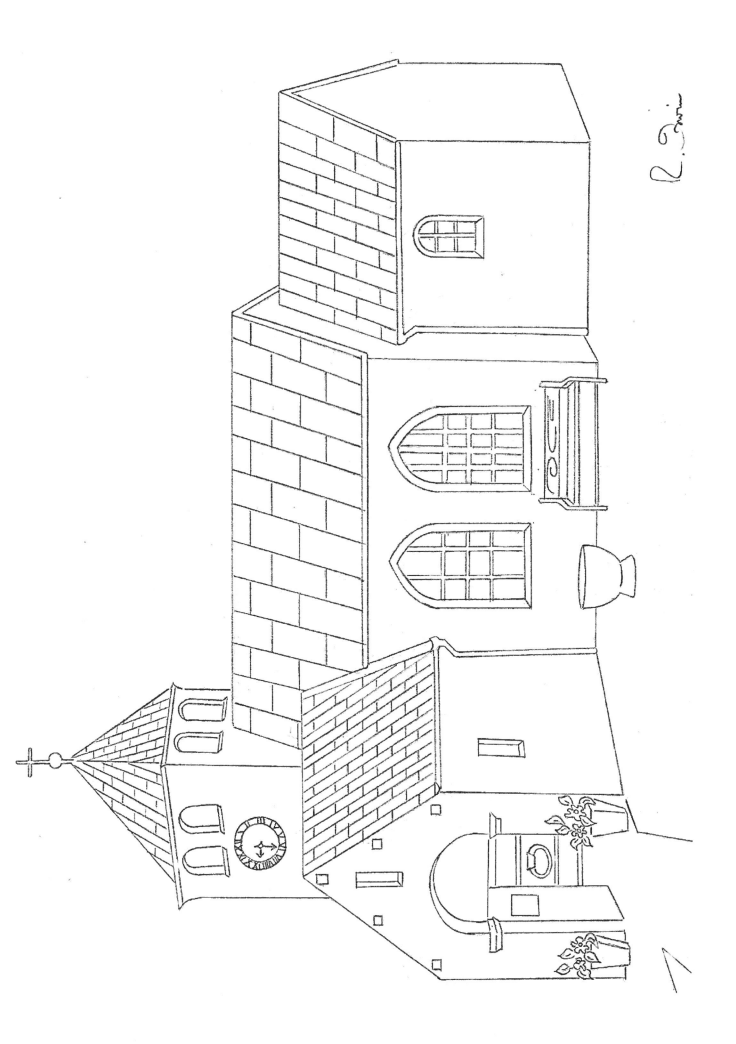

BAMBI

Sad and lonely sat a kitten, cold, abandoned, near a farm;
When a kind girl suddenly found her,
And asked the burly farmer in the barn:

Kind sir, is this your kitten? "No", he answered, "she is not mine!"
"You may by all means have her, as that would be just fine".
The little girl, delighted! scooped kitty up into her arms,
Tucked her into her winter coat, kitty snuggled up, felt warm.

We named her little "Bambi", She was a scrawny, fragile cat,
Soon "Bambi" won the hearts of all; and that thus settled that.
When taken to the vet, he said; that she would not survive,
She'd had a fall, broken her hip, needed surgery to stay alive.

He could not give a guarantee, that Bambi would be fine,
The only other option was: to put her down, in time.
But mother chose to pray for her, and keep her comfortable instead,
Kept her warm and fed her well, in her very own special bed.

Soon Bambi started to hobble, the pain seemed to have eased;
Bambi then began to walk about, with a swagger, that just pleased.
Soon well again and sprightly, she grew and played with us,
We bought her toys; to her delight, she purrs, enjoys the fuss.

A happy, healthy cat now, she enjoys her home and space,
Watches "Countryfile" on television,
Healed! Now Bambi is an ace!

R. Irwin

BUG WONDER

A tiny bug lived in a pond, in murky, stagnant waters,
He crawled around the muddy floor, a non-interfering squatter.
He was content with his life in this dirty, smelly place;
Curiosity got his attention, when he saw:
A tall reed, growing in his space.

Gripping on for dear life, slowly climbing up the stalk;
Hovering above in the distance, he could see a squawking hawk.
He tottered for a moment, but steadied himself again,
He wondered what life must be like;
In the sunshine and the rain.

On he plodded steadily, never looking down.
He was an ugly looking critter; muddy and dark brown.
Bug felt a little different, as he moved towards the top;
Somehow a little lighter, he'd grown a tail that flopped.

Reaching to the top, he paused; so breath-taking was the view,
I'm never going back down he thought: I love the light and hues.
He sat in awe, just gawking; at the beautiful sounds and things.
When suddenly he realised; he had grown beautiful, transparent wings.

He looked down at his body, and everything seemed to glow,
He gasped! At the turquoise blue he'd turned, he never figured how.
Look! A beautiful dragonfly! A child pointed out at him;
He'd never heard his name before,
But it sounded good and prim.

BUTTERCUPS

Buttercups are golden yellow; flowers in the woods,
They're cheerful and they're happy, almost smiling, if they could.
On sunny days in springtime, see them glowing all around;
Near ponds, in parks, out in the fields, they always can be found.

These tiny little flowers, so beautiful and bright;
They shimmer in the sunlight, like radiant, shining lights.
Six hundred different species, a variety; almost like gens,
Most common: the creeping Buttercup; 'Ranunculus repens.'

To determine if you like butter; just hold one to your chin,
The shiny yellow petals, will cause a mild reflection.
They grow wild in many places, and are poisonous to eat,
"Wash your hands, after you've touched them", of this, I do entreat!

R. Irvin

CATERPILLAR CONVERSION

The caterpillar crawled and ate, until he got so fat,
A voracious, greedy eater; he was so good at that.
He crept into a tiny space, among the leaves, so green;
Spun a cocoon around himself, so he could not be seen.

Obeying his DNA instructions, that he had to keep;
He yawned and curled into a ball, and then he fell asleep.
Knowing not, how time flew by; he stirred, stretched and wriggled;
He suddenly discovered, that he was different as he wiggled.

Peeping out from his cocoon, he then tried to crawl outside;
Instead these colourful wings emerged, radiant on either side.
Butterfly wings that flapped around! Which he could not understand;
Hurrah! He spread his wings and flew, to a land just far beyond.

CHARMING CHILDREN

Two delightful little children, one eight, the other four;
From Solbjerg came to visit, their Grandma, they call "Mormor".
Charming little children, with good manners, and polite;
On their very best behaviour, they were an absolute delight.

Beautiful in looks and friendly, they instantly touched my heart;
Even though language was a barrier, tight from the very start.
We played a game of football, that had no set of rules,
England versus Denmark; like a bunch of kids in school.

We screamed, laughed and kicked the ball,
It was such jolly fun, language of love to communicate,
It must have sounded weird to some.
Flowerpots marked boundaries, of where the goals should be.
While Lise cooked delicious food, we laughed and played so free.

COFFEE

A special kind of "Coffee"; not the usual one we know.
She is a beautiful Dalmatian, who is always on the go.
Her greetings are a special one; as she smiles and shows her teeth,
She wags her tail with fervour, at those she loves to greet.

Pretty spots of brown are dotted, along her soft white furry coat,
She likes to go a sailing, on the ocean, in a boat.
Playing ball is different, as she doesn't know how to fetch,
So be prepared to retrieve the ball to exercise and stretch.
She is affectionate and faithful, obedient as can be;
All until she sees a cat, or a deer or two maybe.

DRAGONFLIES

Dragon flies have compound eyes right atop their heads.
Two pairs of brightly coloured wings, and three pairs of spiny legs.
Dragon flies are 'ectotherms', and can fire up their wings;
Using rapid whirring movements, they are very clever little things.

This warms their tiny bodies; they have built in survival skills.
One wonders if like humans, they have persistent will.
Transparent wings are like reflectors soaking solar energy up,
They can deflect the sunshine, when it is too hot.

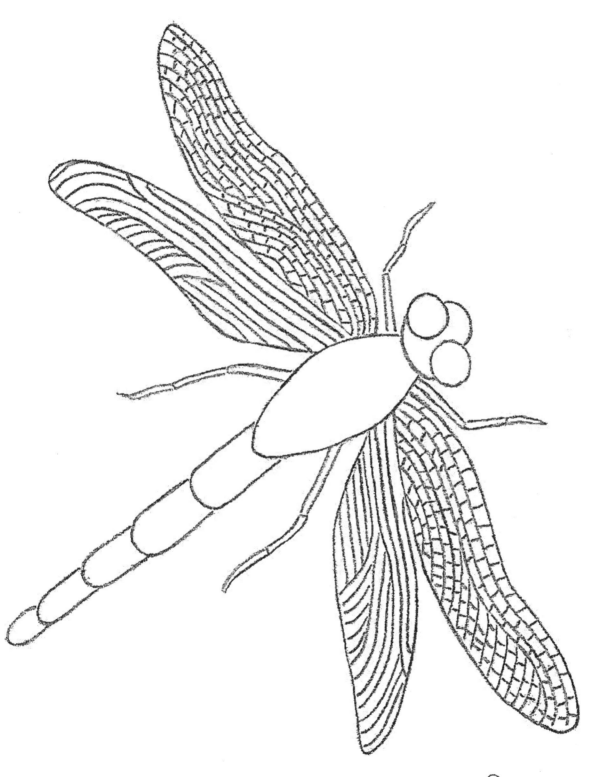

R. Sim

ESTHER AND JOANNA
WONDERFUL CHILDREN

Gentle, loving, beautiful and kind, simple at heart with innocent minds.
At the age of two, they recited Psalms; at prayer times,
difficult times, to quell and calm.

Intelligent, precious, dearest ones; daughters bold! Equivalent to sons!
Psalm ninety-one recited word for word, spoken aloud, believed and heard.
In troubled times, in distant lands, each word comforting, strengthening bonds.
Barefooted they just loved to play, on the mountainside throughout the day.

Always teaching them; I watched them grow, let God's words of wisdom overflow,
Into their precious, beautiful souls; to keep them safe, make them feel whole.
Words of wisdom do impart, a strength that forms inner ramparts.

Enhancing endurance in upheaval,
To be excellent at what they do, be innocent of evil.
Now into fine young ladies; they have grown,
Professionals, with individual characters of their own.

Kindness brimming, compassion flows, as beacons of light, constantly aglow.
Confident, caring in all they do, serving humanity, sincere and true,
Bringing hope to all they meet. To the poor, mediocre or the elite.

To pets, creatures great and small
Kindness and love extended to them all.
Blessed to be a blessing here,
May they excel in all things and never doubt or fear.

FAMILIES

Families are precious people, connected here on earth,
Different cultures and generations, simplified by human birth.
Genetics complicated; genomes specified;
Unfathomable interactions, complexly categorised.

Blood types may always vary, yet components never change,
Whatever generation, there's no reason to estrange.
Variant race or colour of the skin of any person,
The same Life is in the blood of all; thus it is for certain.

Some look alike, some do alike. We're smart and fancy folk.
Some comical, some serious, some live life as a joke.
Whatever situations are, we're meant to stick together,
Like instinctive flocks of birds that are of particular feather.

Charming, grumpy, happy, content, all kinds of diverse spirits,
That is correct! We are flesh bodies, with a spirit in it.
Some get along and others don't, it really doesn't matter.
What matters most is tolerance, love and forgiveness scattered.

Each one unique, brilliant, and smart, we are the human race;
Our sizes are all variant, with Master crafted special faces.
Respect, protect each dear one, must be our candid aim,
Supporting on to glory or propelling on to fame.

Generations come and go, yet DNA persists,
Trace families from long ago, connect kith and kin, a myth.
Our destinies defined by One, The Creator of all time,
The human race, in time and space in Him are all sublime.

FRIENDSHIP

Choose every friendship wisely, friends are a family we choose,
Treasure and make them feel special, spend time, respect their views.
Friends are never selfish, never harsh, never unkind.
True friendships bring security, enduring a lifetime.

Lives intertwined intriguingly, so powerfully connected.
No matter what the circumstance; can never be disconnected.
Precious bonds of friendships, invisible cords of love;
That spans the years, it's timeless; blessed from heaven above.

GLOW WORMS

Female glow worms, glow brightly, to attract the flying mates;
Bright as LED indicators, their glow is in their tail.
'Lampyris noctiluca'; more common, than we could ever think,
They lay their eggs, turn out their lights, their lives are on the brink.

Fourteen to twenty-one days or so, their life spans are very short,
Adult glow worms can't feed at all, they'll die, if they are caught.
They thrive in specialised habitats, so do not take them home,
From late May to early September, you can see them as you roam.

The adult male is smaller, he rarely even glows,
Six legs, two wings; is what he has,
These things we ought to know.
A molecule called 'Luciferin', oxidises to produce:
Oxyluciferin; with luciferase as catalyst.

This bioluminescence is more efficient than our lights.
Tiny glow worms are insects; a very fascinating sight.
Just like the little glow worms, we shine as bright lights too,
In thoughts, actions, words, kind deeds in all we say and do.

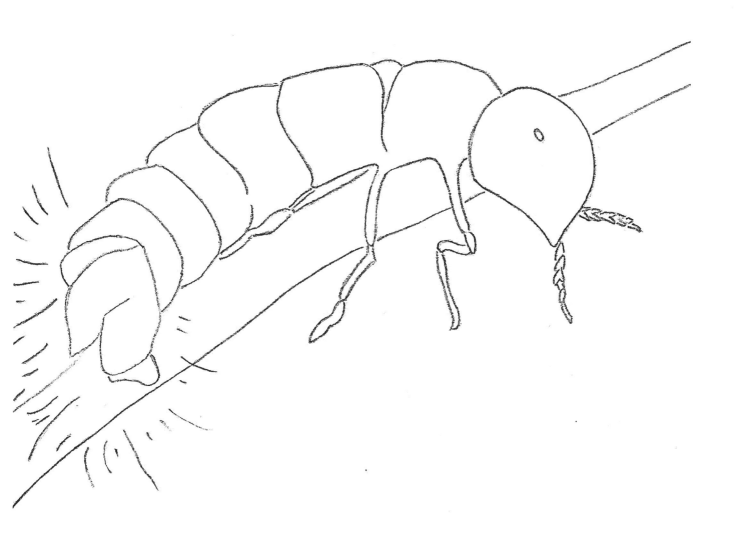

GOOD ATTITUDE

Be kind to every fellow being, in actions, words or deeds;
Spread laughter, joy and happiness, these are a kind of seeds.
It will soon become contagious, as a smile lights up each face,
Love always triumphs over hate; makes the world a better place.

Lend helping hands and learn to share,
With those who aren't as fortunate,
Be diligent in all you do,
Honest, sympathetic and compassionate.
Every person is so precious, no matter who they may be.
Treat everyone as equally; that's how we live in harmony.

Individuals are all different, two people are never the same;
Yet the goal to live amicably; is our focus and our aim.
Respectful to opinions, let each one have their say;
A good attitude helps everyone, we encounter every day.

GRASSHOPPERS

Grasshoppers are insects, locusts; that leap hop and fly.
They are coloured brightly, grey or green;
Have you ever wondered why?
Rubbing their legs and wings together, they make an awful sound,
They're found in countries everywhere,
In the whole world, all around.

The females have pointed abdomens, and lay eggs underground.
They blend into the environment, wherever they are found.
Living in fields and meadows, they voraciously eat plants.
They spit at their predators; or quickly disappear, when they can't.

These herbivorous insects, in large amounts, are pests;
They have chewing mouthparts, and have an eating zest.
They are a source of protein; some people eat them too;
'John the Baptist', in the Bible, with honey, ate a few.

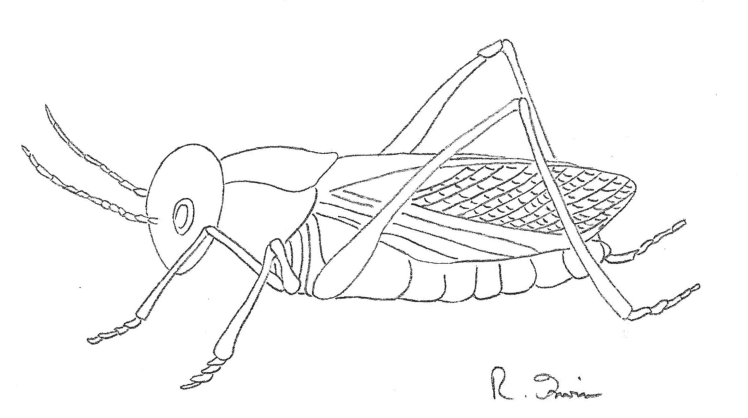

R. Brian

HUMBLE BUMBLE

Beautiful Bumble bee, yellow and brown,
One day, had a sad face, and began to frown.
His friends had said: he was ugly and fat,
His wings were too tiny; though he never thought that.

Aerodynamics confirmed; that he never would fly,
But beautiful Bumble could never think why.
His Maker, Creator, had commanded him to;
So trusting, in faith, he spread his wings and he flew.

Whenever discouraging words, cause dismay,
Don't dwell on the negative things, people may say.
There is special potential, put inside everyone;
So make every effort to get your work done.

IN THE MOONLIGHT

In the light of the moon, there's a soft shining glow;
And the shimmer on dew drops, creates a silvery flow.
A glimmer in the twilight, a sparkle on the dew;
These things so very few enjoy, in the shadows of the Yew.
Tall giant like, strong evergreens, create a daunting sight;
Their shadows cast some eerie shapes, on a silvery moonlit night.

Night creatures stealthily come alive, darting shadows can be seen,
Their beady eyes shine steadily, hunting prey with eyes that gleam.
Gentle sounds of lapping water, soothes the senses, brings a calm;
As the river runs persistently, over rocks with sounds that charm.
There's beauty in the moonlight, there's beauty all around;
Fascinating dancing shadows, even beauty in the sounds.

LADYBIRDS

Have you ever seen a ladybird? People call them "bugs".
They're incredible tiny insects, that look so smart and smug.
Technically they're beetles, with teeny hard red shells;
Black spotted, plain, or even striped, observe, differentiate and tell.

Five thousand species in the world, Family of Coccinellidae,
Yellow, orange, brown, pink or black, identifiable this way.
Greatest allies of farmers, loved by gardeners,
These pretty little ladybirds, are voracious carnivores.

They eat the dreaded aphids: insects, which are pests;
They also eat the fruit flies, devouring them with zest.
During the Middle Ages, aphids were destroying crops;
Europeans prayed to Virgin Mary, sought help for this to stop.

Soon tiny insects descended, to the aphids they were lethal,
Grateful farmers named them, "Our Lady's miracle beetles"!
The ladybird's bright colours, are important for their defence;
Reminding their predators, they taste disgusting foul and dense.

They secrete an oily, yucky fluid, from joints within their legs,
Their spots warn potential predators;
When threatened, they play dead.

See them in spring or summer, crawling or flitting about,
Laying eggs in aphid colonies, they're clever ones, no doubt.
Harlequin, Harmonia axyridis, Eyed ladybird, Cream spot!
Mexican bean, Squash beetles, Orange, Kidney spot, all sorts!

Numerous interesting species, they thrive in colonies,
Hibernating in the winter, under rocks, rotting logs or trees.
It supposedly brings good luck, if one alights and sits on you,
Ladybirds are charming, enjoy their colours and their hues.

LEGO LAND

A grand entrance gate at Lego land, to a fascinating place.
On a hot and sunny summers day, we went in shorts and lace.
The Danish flag, majestically, stood tall above the crowds,
In the sweltering heat, a fun day out; in the skies above, no clouds.

Miniature buildings, airport, hotels, the station and the mall,
The Eiffel tower, and the Shard, in Lego bricks stood tall.
Giant roller coaster rides, Vikings made of coloured bricks,
French hot dogs and snacks, cold ice-creams on a stick.

We talked, walked, bought souvenirs,
Key rings, fridge magnets, shirts.
Miles we walked in Lego land,
At Billund, on the outskirts.

Inside the 'haunted house' was dark,
Strange noises, shrieks were heard.
Creepy ghost like figures,
Skeletons and nerds.

Penguins swam in large tanks, sharks in the aquarium;
Like children, we enjoyed it all, joyous delirium!
Exhausted, in the stifling heat, we sat down in the shade;
I soon dozed off as I lay back, on cool grasses in the glade.

LIFE

New beginnings, new horizons, new adventures in the offing;
Pause a while, regain new strength, surge ahead, there is no stopping.
Life awaits, there's always more; move forward, resilient, be strong.
Accept and be kind, humble, helping hands,
When sometimes things go wrong.

Life is full of fun and joy; it is what each one makes it;
Enrich it, opportunities await, each day live to the fullest.
Every heartbeat is a miracle, life is limited by time,
Embrace and cherish every moment,
Let love and kindness shine.

EVERY HEARTBEAT

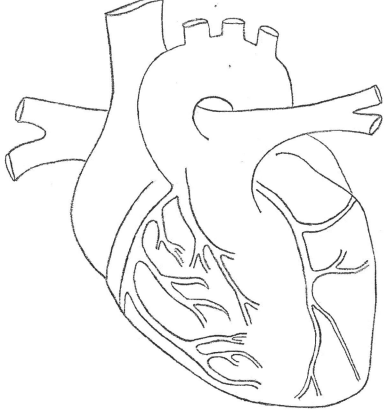

IS A MIRACLE
OF LIFE

R. Irwin

LISE AND ME

Across the deep North Sea, we flew;
A vast expanse, breath taking views.
Welcomed by my dearest childhood friend,
Across the "puddle" 'around the bend'!

Tranquillity! In a perfect place! To meet at last, just face to face.
Time and years, flown by, stood still;
As we hugged we cried, the tears just spilled.

Beautiful sights in Denmark beckoned;
Forty-four years were spanned in seconds.
Treasured moments from the past,
Once more revived, re-lived. A blast!

Catching up with our lives was fun,
The journey re-commenced, had just begun.
Fantastic times just spent together.
Hurray! We survived! Now we're friends forever.

MINDFULNESS

Mindfulness is simple, it's how we think and speak,
Treating others kindly, being gentle, mild and meek.
Be thoughtful in the things we do, loving, sympathetic and kind.
Considerate always in everything; it refreshes, soothes our minds.

Identifying we're different, yet knowing, we are the human race.
Respecting others, and their opinions,
Whatever, the colour of their face.
We are all created special, each one is loved by God,
Unique in every manner, some intelligent, some odd

ODI AND BAMBI

These two adorable creatures, that some of you have met,
Can teach us all some tolerance; even though they are our pets.
Colour, species, or pedigree, matters not to these.
Being vary, yet tolerant, they live side by side; at ease.

We all have many differences, just like this dog and cat,
But we can still live in harmony, almost, somewhat like that.
Becoming friends is vital, it is clear as you can see.
Respecting individuality; enhances unity.

As on the sofa, side by side, these share a common space,
Clearly displaying facts; to choose and tolerate all race.
Our canine, feline friends, without a word, have stated;
That enmity and disharmony, can definitely be outdated.

OYSTER ITCH

Oysters are bi-valve molluscs, living on the ocean floor,
It scavenges and eats the stuff, that others leave below.
Oysters filter water, many gallons each day.
Excellent for the environment, in their own spectacular way.

Oysters do not like rough sand, when washed up on the beach,
It squirms, spits and rolls about in places out of reach.
Poor oyster has a hard time, when sand gets in its belly;
It makes secreting juices, which render it O! So smelly!

But as it thrashes on the ocean floor, to rid the grains of sand,
Beautiful pearls are formed, created; that are harvested on land.
The tiny pearls are awesome! Creamy white and shiny;
Something precious was created from an oyster, so tiny.

Take examples from the oyster, when life gets difficult,
Keep calm, become a precious pearl,
Ignore the hurts and insults.

PONDER THE CHRISTMAS STORY

In the stillness of the night, at the stable, all is quiet;
A baby's cry is heard on earth; a Saviour is born of Royal birth.
In a humble manger, full of hay, in an earthly cradle, there He lay.
He took the form of human seed; He came to fulfil our every need.

The star in the east, it shone so bright, on a cold and starry, winter's night.
Wise men had followed from afar, this guiding light, this unusual star.
They travelled at night, to a destination unknown;
Paid homage to a child, they had not known.
Yet faith in God requires trust, they followed the star, because they must.

Laid their treasures at His feet, gave, to a baby boy, so meek.
These rich wise men, where did they stay?
As they travelled dusty roads along the way.

They focused on this astounding light;
That dispelled the darkness in their plight.
Shepherds, who heard the angel voices,
Then had to make some professional choices:

Tend the sheep or follow the Saviour?
Obey instructions, to see a baby in a manger?
Such strange events, as the Christmas story unfolds,
Ponder, accept, and obey His Majesty, as the tale is re-told.

'Bright Morning Star', behold! He is here,
Jesus the King forever is near.
Not a child anymore, but a beautiful Saviour;
Accept Him today, receive His Grace and His favour.

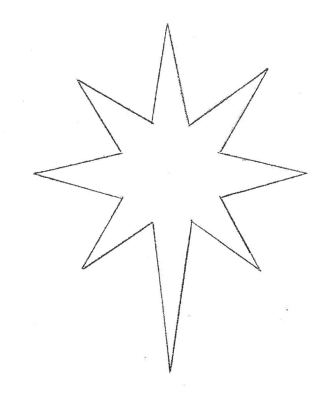

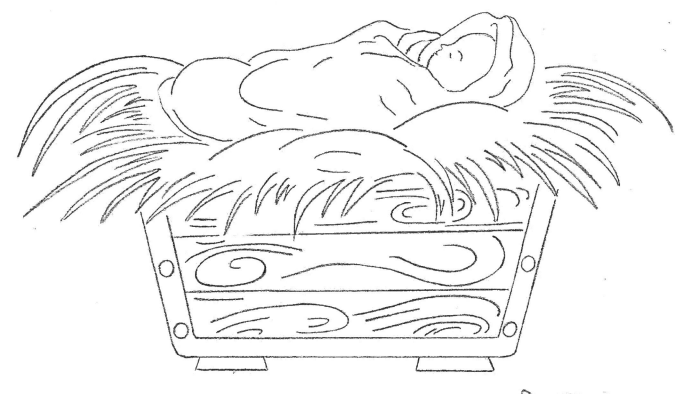

POSITIVE DECLARATIONS

I am beautiful (good looking), intelligent, I'm brilliant and wise,
I'm loving, kind, compassionate; and not defined by size.
I am smart, and I'm invincible, I am wonderfully made.
No matter what the world may say, I shall never be afraid.

I am all things good and well, resilient and strong.
I am loved by friends and family,
Even when things go wrong.

My purpose: to praise God and love, my goals are intuitive.
My passions, my desires, correspond inchoative.
I am "God's treasured possession", though I may feel differently;
I do believe I'm special, because I am apparently.

I can do everything I purpose to,
I am not deterred by trials;
By God's grace, I'm supernatural!
In a human vessel, or this 'vial'.

Whatever be my circumstance,
Or all that life may throw my way;
Like a buoy upon the ocean,
Peacefully; I will just say:

"This too shall pass, and all is well, it's soon another day.
A fresh start, a new beginning,
New opportunities, Hurray!"

SPEAK YOUR
BLESSINGS
INTO EXISTENCE;
BY SAYING
POSITIVE
WORDS
ONLY!

R. Irwin

SHIPS

Like ships upon the ocean,
We sail life's stormy seas,
While billows roll and it is dark,
Encountering difficulties.

Majestically with sails unfurled,
Keep sailing on in time,
This too shall pass, and storms abate,
All soon will be sublime.

Meanwhile stay strong, take courage,
Don't disrupt a beautiful life,
The power is within each one,
To discard negative words and strife.

Don't let the water get into your ship,
Circumstances don't determine one's fate,
Sail on into the calmer zones,
Stay focused, quell despair, equate.

We never sail alone in life,
"The Captain" sails with us,
Though unaware that He exists;
He is our Creator, our truss.

R. Irwin

SIGNETS

The signets have arrived at last
Delightful as can be,
As they swim along majestically,
They're a beautiful sight to see.

Under watchful eyes of their parents,
They skim along the lake
They're learning their survival skills,
In the journey of life to partake.

Sometimes jostling for attention,
They ride on their mother's back;
Perched between her feathers
Protected, safe from any attack.

SLUGS

Slugs are Gastropod mollusc, that do not have a shell,
In different colours and varieties, their faces are grotesque.
Limax Cinereoniger, has a pale-yellow keel,
All along its slithery back, from its head to its tail.

This slimy Ashy grey slug, the largest when fully grown;
Up to twenty-five centimetres long, mature woodlands are their home.
Arion distinctus; the common garden slug,
In northern England, Ireland, in Scotland, in the bog.

Brown in colour, striped lengthwise, it has shiny orange mucus,
An orange belly underside, to identify, just focus.
These are relatively small ones, and are difficult to spot,
Found on agricultural land, do serious damage to the crops.

Slugs are slimy creatures, that live in moisture laden homes,
They cannot thrive in arid land, for it is their danger zone.
Identify their species, from their colour and their size,
Some are hazardous to crops, others exist in different guise.

Banana slug and leopard slug, they all have different names,
All these are Gastropod mollusc, yet they are not the same.
Ugly as they may seem to be, these are important little creatures,
Providing food for birds and mammals;
Recycling matter is their special feature.

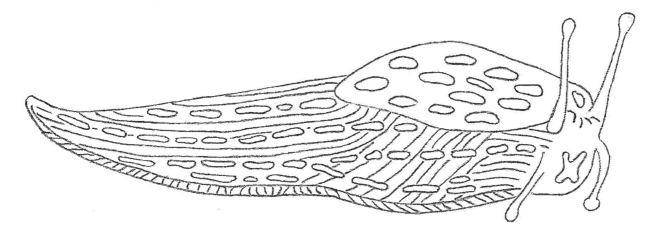
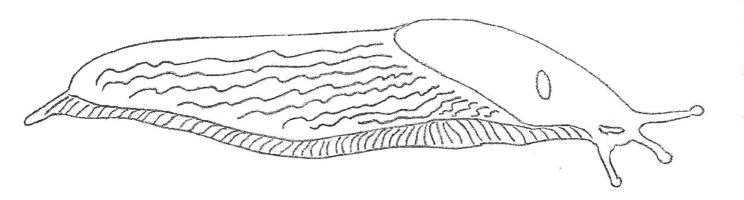

SNOWDROPS

Intriguing delicate flowers, so simple in form;
Shades of green and white, on a cold winter's morn.
A gleaming snow blanket, on trees, grass and stones.
While we snuggle inside, in the warmth of our homes.

Beautiful Snowdrops, tiny and strong,
Withstand the harsh weather, ice, winds and snowstorms.
Whatever the outcome, they survive, and they thrive,
Bringing joy to humans, just for a while.

A peek inside, these tiny flowers,
Reveals fascinating, shades of colour.
Creamy white, and pastel green;
Hidden in the depths, unseen.

Linger, watch, the Snowdrops sway,
On delicate stalks, along the way.
A silent message of hope, they speak;
To those who need comfort, and feel weak.

'Shine on in beauty, in life, through the storms,
Sunshine, love, faith and hope, strengthens at dawn'.
Their gently bowing pose, represents submission,
Their short journey on earth, has a 'cheering' mission.

Silently encouraging, appearing calm and serene,
White pearly shapes, awesome and pristine.
Un-complaining they glow, in the frost and the snow.
So please stop and admire! Because Snowdrops inspire.

THE CROOKED TREE

Like a giant Caterpillar
Or a massive Centipede;
This crooked tree grows humbly
Bowed in form, pose and cede.

Compelling one to focus,
It somehow grasps our attention,
Like a magical creature
From an alien dimension.

Encouraging the viewer,
It gives one strength to see,
This flourishing, resilient,
Disfigured, twisted tree.

A zest for life demonstrated;
It quietly grows strong,
Surely encouraging many people,
That leisurely walk along.

THE ROSE

A quest, for knowledgeable scholars; debating reference to a simple flower.
A dilemma over centuries, discussed, researched, seeking its power.
An enigmatic statement in the Bible, gave this humble flower distinction.
Is it categorised as Rosacea? Or a hibiscus from that region?

These beautiful, fragrant flowers have a scent that is divine,
Significant and meaningful, when crushed they make new wine.
So humble in origin, medicinal qualities in 'Rosehip' form.
Mild tasting fresh Rose water, or sensational essential oil.

Who is this 'Rose of Sharon? Or the 'Lily of the valley?
Consider, ponder, and seek the answer for yourself. Come tarry!
A challenge to be thoughtful, discovering new strength;
The answer will surprise you; be filled with Joy at length.

TIME

We are all given the gift of time,
To live our lives on earth;
Each one's share of it is different,
Commencing at our births.

Specific amounts to each of us,
Whether great or small;
We must make moments special,
And maximize it all.

Too precious to be wasted,
Life cannot be re-lived,
Make sure you leave a legend,
Share time, live well and give.

Kindness, compassion, friendliness,
Are acts of time, well spent.
Sweet memories will linger on,
When time is fulfilled at length.

TRAIN JOURNEY TO KATHGODAM

The engine whistled loudly, smoke belched, from its steamer,
Tiny nose, pressed to the window; I was that little dreamer.
In the light of dawn; dark mountains loomed;
Majestically, in the distance;
An exciting journey, for the first time;
Glorious views, at every instance.

On the narrow-gauge line, this smaller train, chugged happily along;
The 'clickety-clack' of wheels on rails, seemed a cheerful song.
Mother sat beside me, after packing all our bags,
And rolling up the 'hold-all's', with our names written on the tags.

Our black metal trunks, tucked away under the benches,
A tiny metal suitcase, The 'tuck-box'; crammed with all essentials.
'Lalkuan jaleebies'! Morning delicacies, to savour,
A steaming cup of 'chai', that had a ginger-cardamom flavour.

Seats on the train in second class, were hard planks of wood;
The sleeper coach or first-class coupe:
One booked, whatever they could.
Alas! Affordability! Was the criteria, to how one travelled.
Though it never seemed to matter much,
As the awesome scenery, unravelled.

The little train was painted blue, in a light and darker shade;
With tiny, square, glass windows, in a rather splendid façade.
The 'chai wallas' at the stations, with kettle and stacks of teacups;
'Chai garam!' said a quirky voice, awakening sleepy travellers up.

One could alight at Haldwani, and take a taxi onwards,
Up the winding, scenic, treacherous roads;
To Nainital and homewards.
We travelled on to Kathgodam, quite cosy on the train;
The weather front was cold outside, with freezing, icy rain.

Two steam engines moved the train, over rugged, harsh terrain.
One pushed, the other pulled; simplicity in this domain.
The train chugged into the station; Kathgodam, at last!

Alighting on the platform;
These are, pleasant memories from the past!
It's good to be a dreamer, pursue in life, and progress;
Your quest with zest ongoing, will soon achieve success.

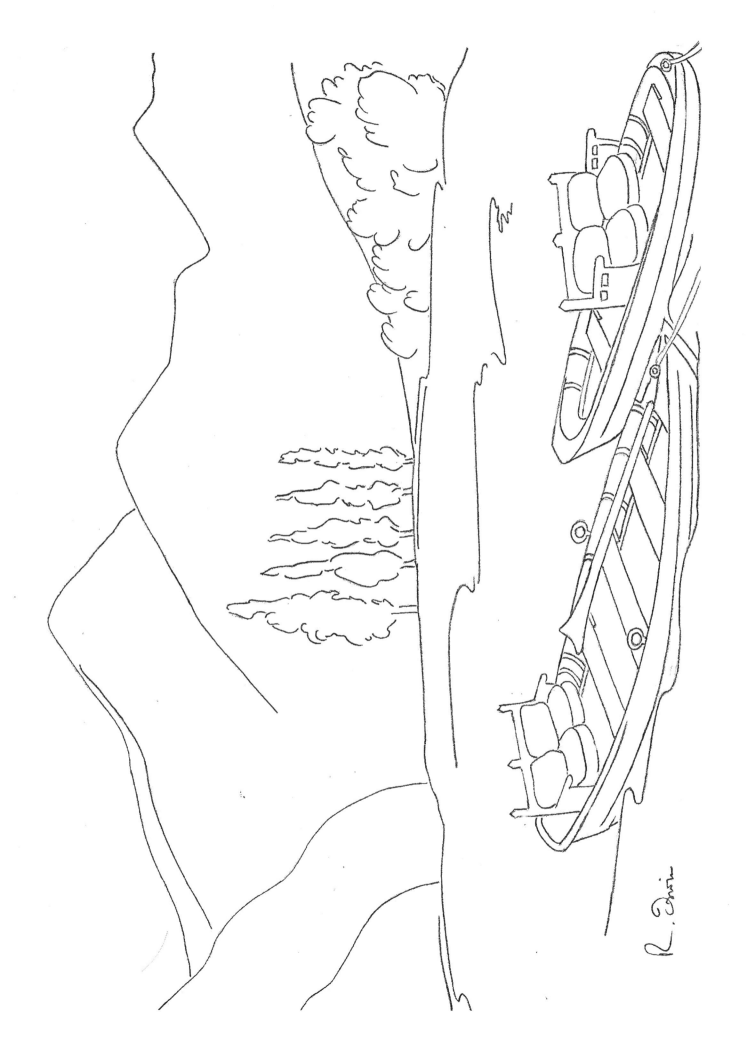

HVIDE SANDE (WHITE SANDS)

She drove her car with expertise, from 'Give' down to the beach;
Along some picturesque country roads, until 'Hvide Sands' we reached.
Rolling farmlands, tall Fir trees, bales of hay in white;
Cows, all grazing lazily, with wind turbines in sight.

Her white hat with pretty ribbon, I wore upon my head,
Under my chin it fastened, with silky, fine twined thread.
July the twenty-sixth it was, a bright and sunny day,
Two friends now re-united, in a delightful, beautiful way.

Walking along the soft wet sand, we stopped along the shore;
We talked, laughed, picked pebbles up; our lives enriched once more.
Delicious homemade sandwiches, we ate from a cool lunch box;
Drank beer and flavoured water, as waves lapped upon the rocks.

Sitting on a picnic blanket, gazing at the sea,
Waves shimmering in the sunshine,
While a ship sailed majestically!

WORDS

Words have electro-magnetic frequencies, they're filled with sound and light,
Powerful yet invisible, creating patterns, forming unimaginable delights.
Words are supernatural, as they have no form or shape;
Yet possess the power to impact on fragile lives; almost like a swape.

Words reach into the unseen world, and they create and form;
Each spoken word has energy to bring peace or whip up a storm.
Some words are hurtful, others are kind; we get to choose each day.
Spread love or hate, sow peace or discord; it's all in what we say.

Speak kind and gentle words each day, create a future bright,
Words we utter here today, for sure determines all forthright.
Ponder each thought before you speak, consider the effects of sound,
Once spoken aloud in form of words, like echoes, each rebounds.

"The Word of Life" our Creator, empowers every spoken word,
Endowing each with energy, impacting like a sword.
Choose carefully, each word you speak, reshape a broken, hurting world;
Kindness in sound just resonates, a flag of peace it unfurls.

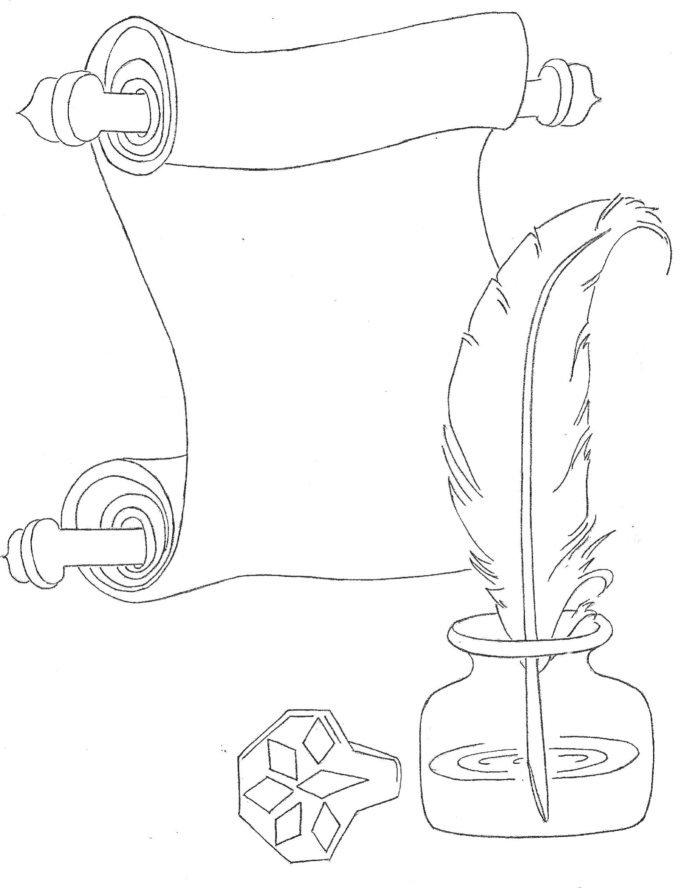

R. Irwin

JOIN

THE

DOTS

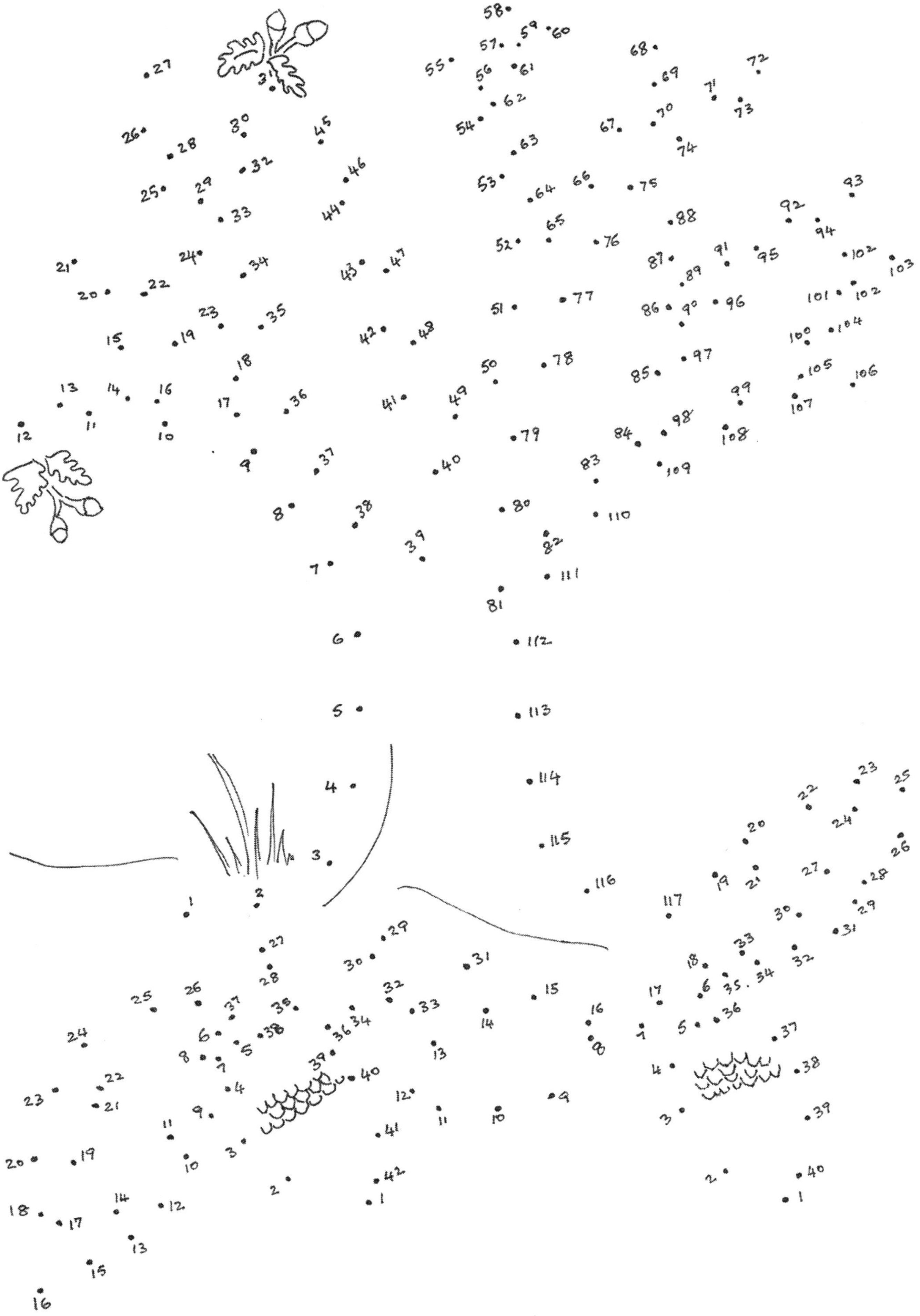

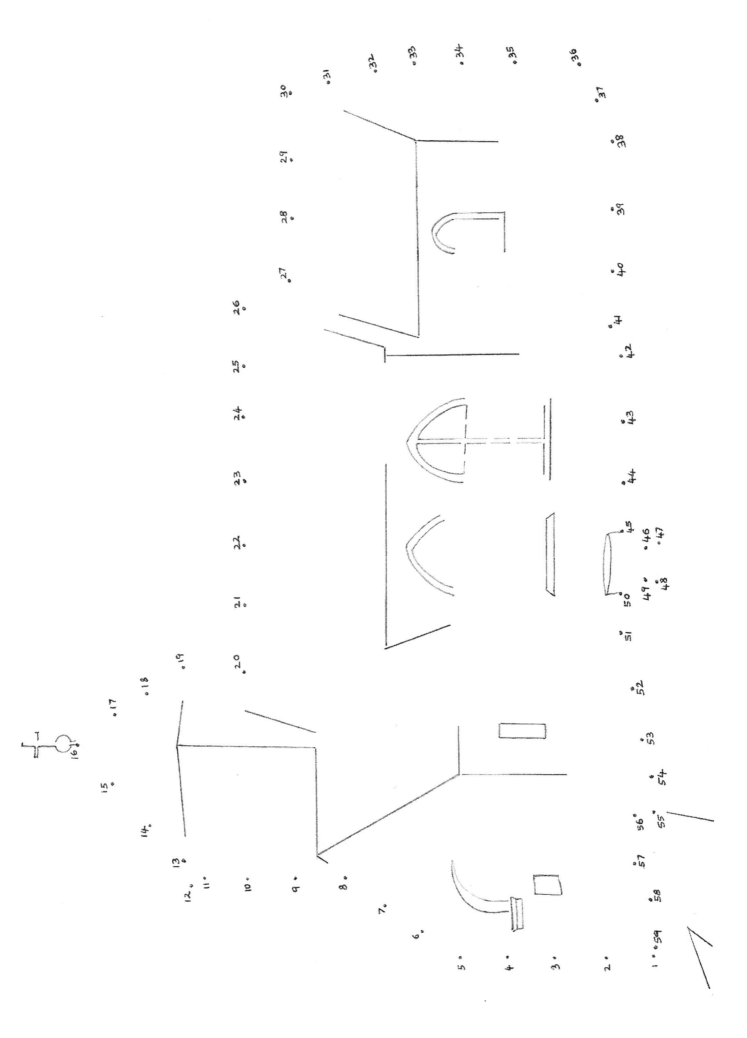

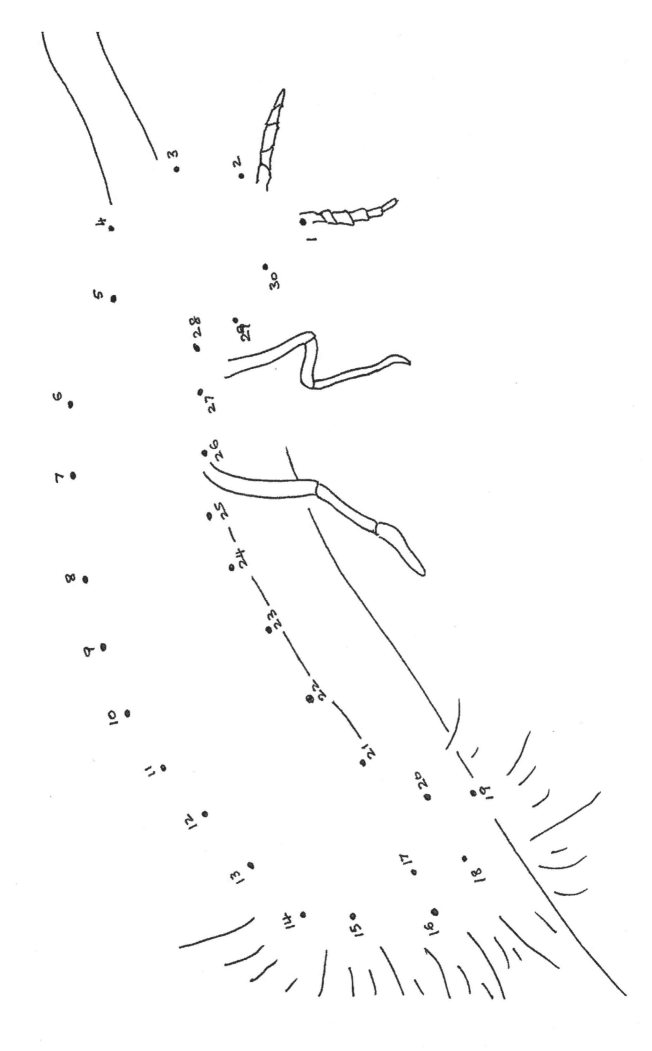

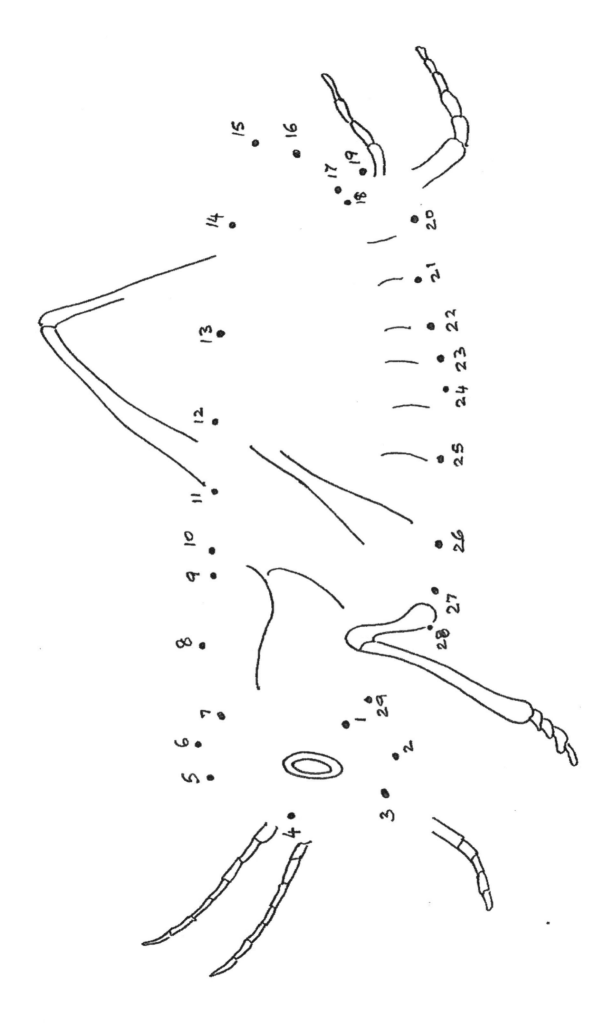

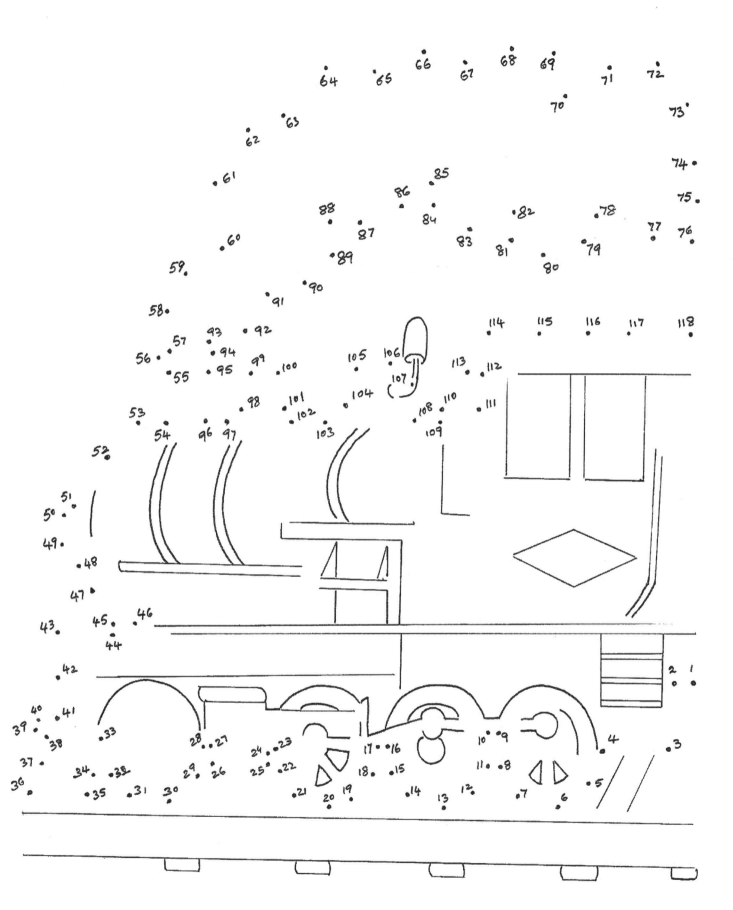

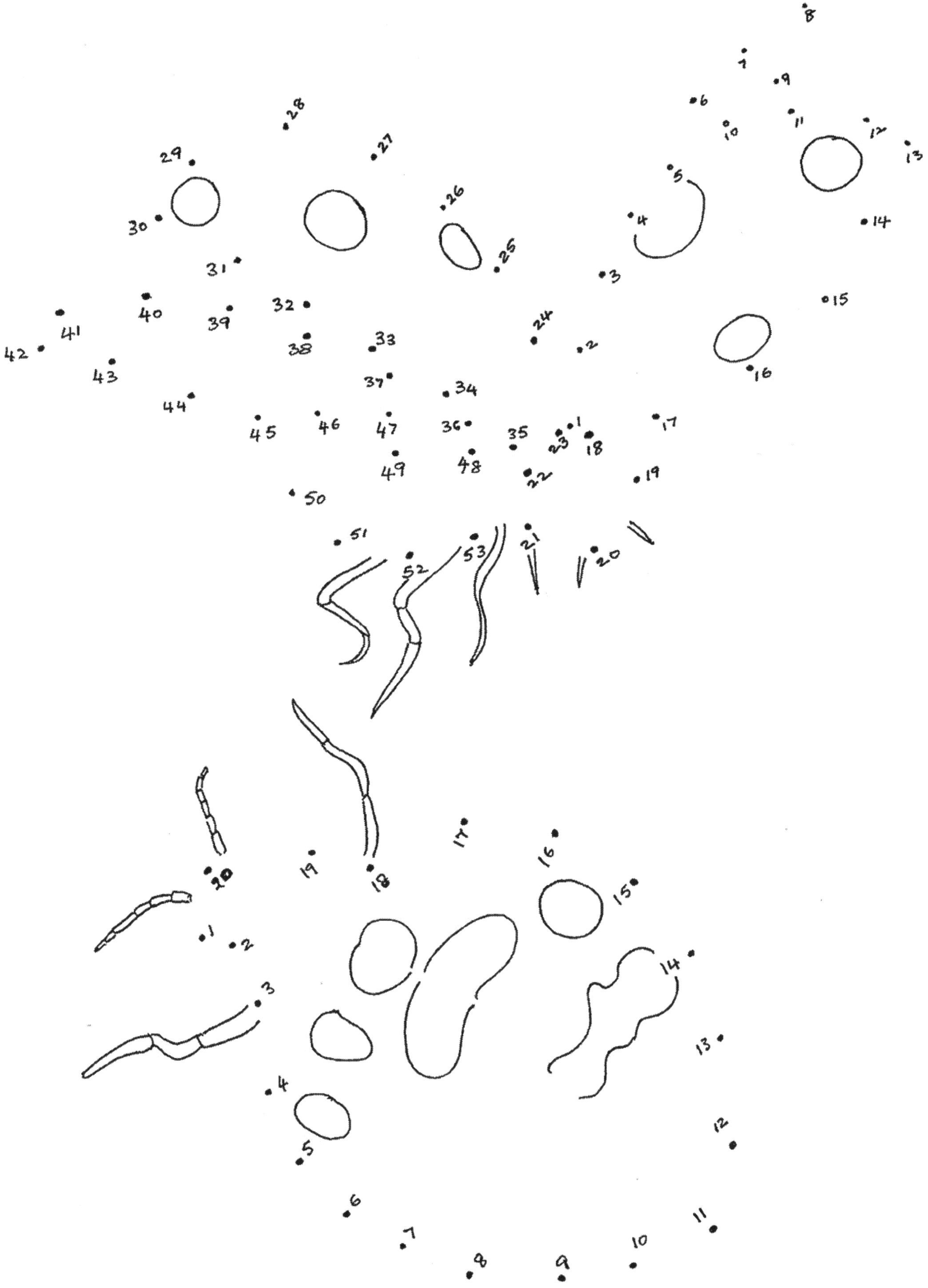

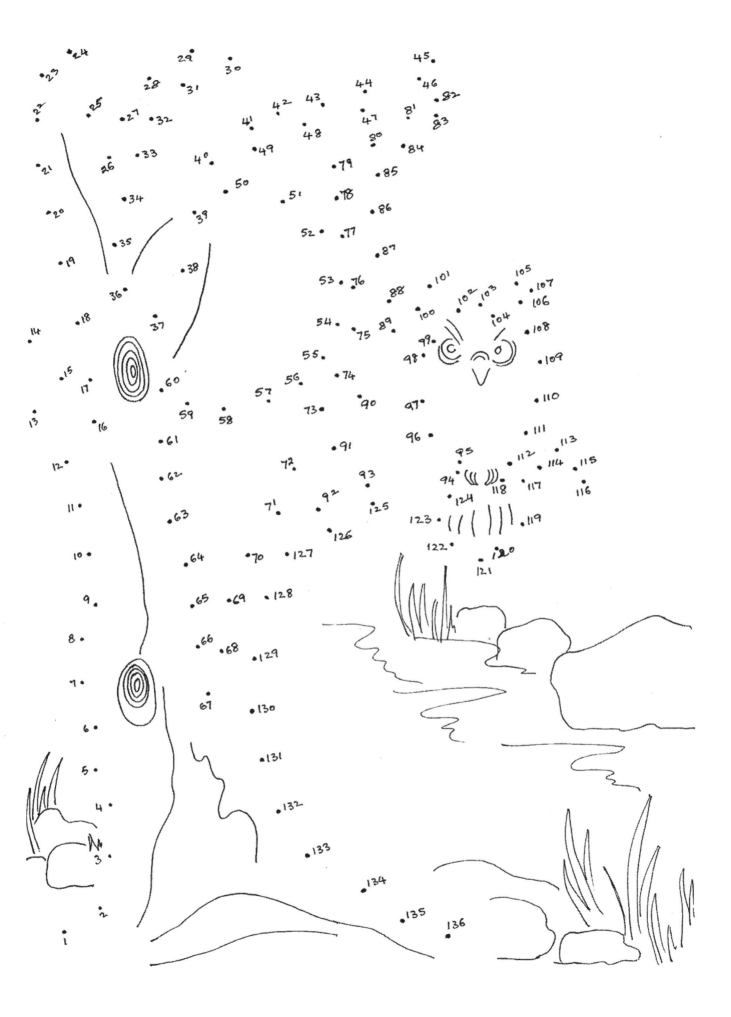

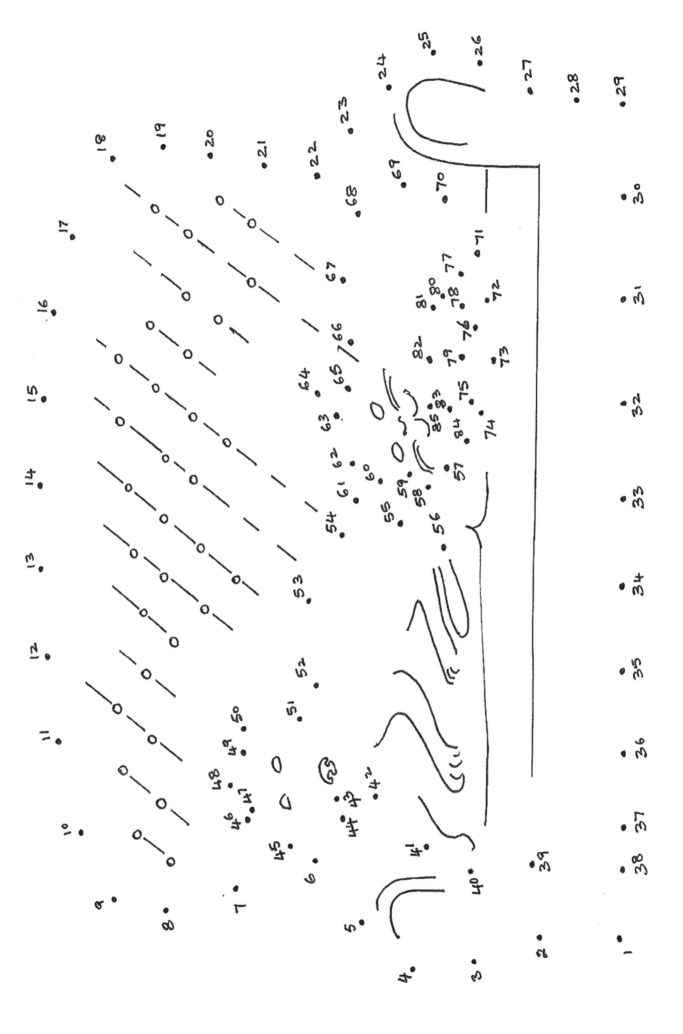

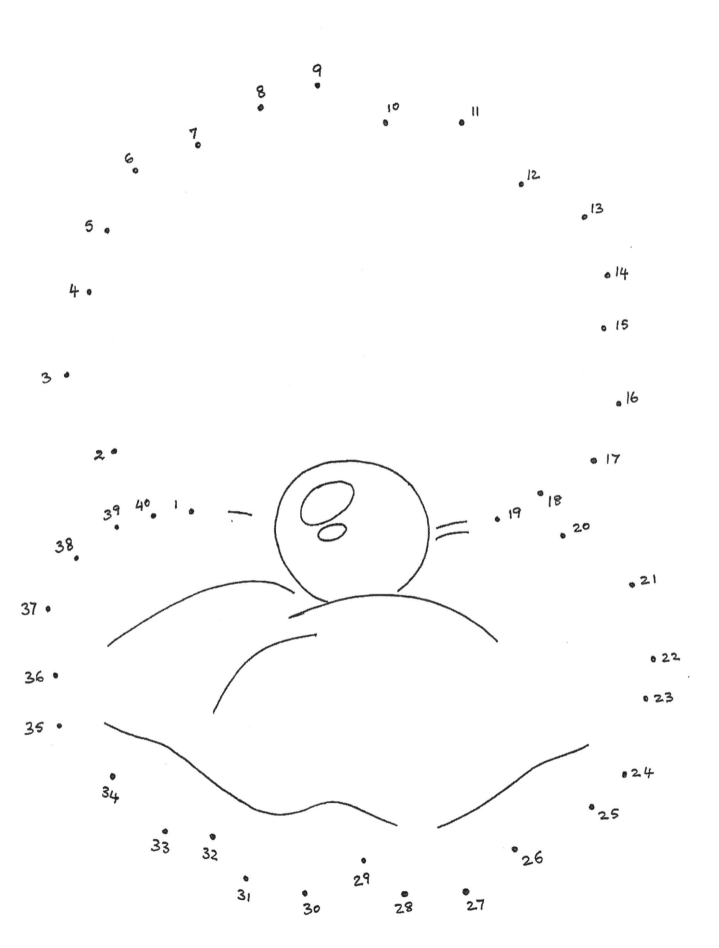

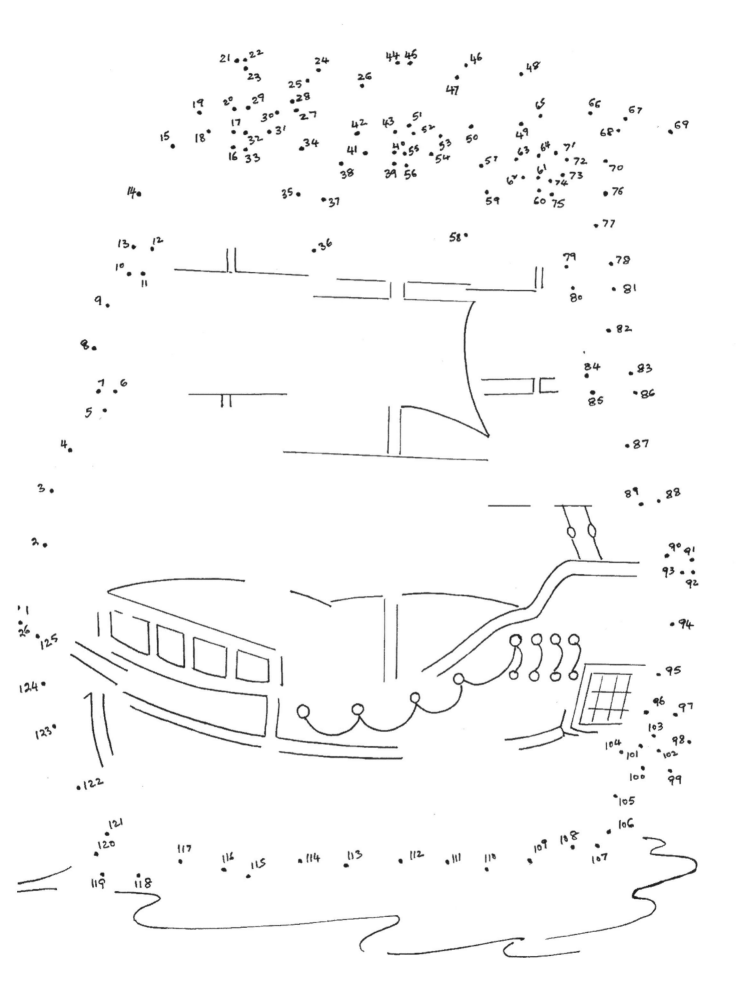

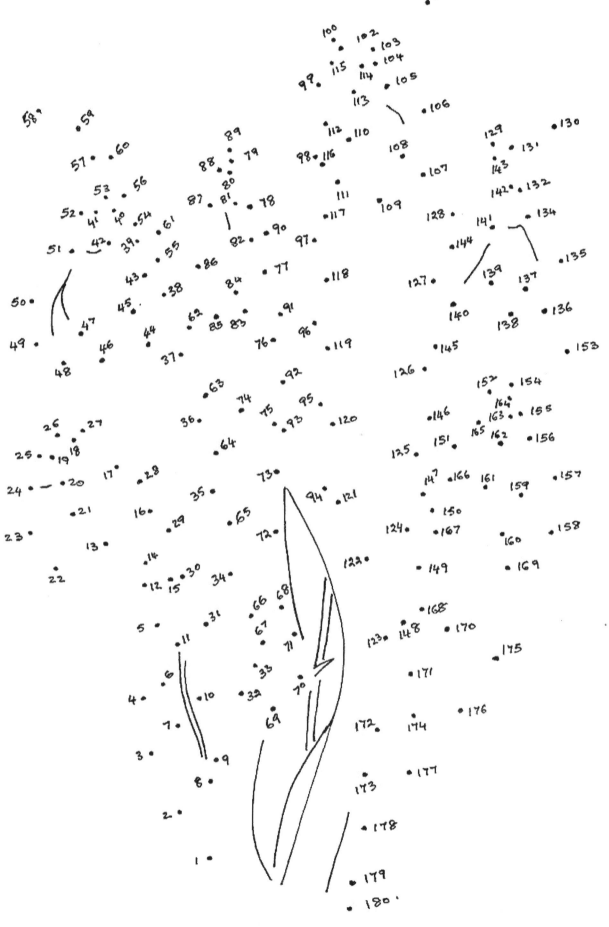

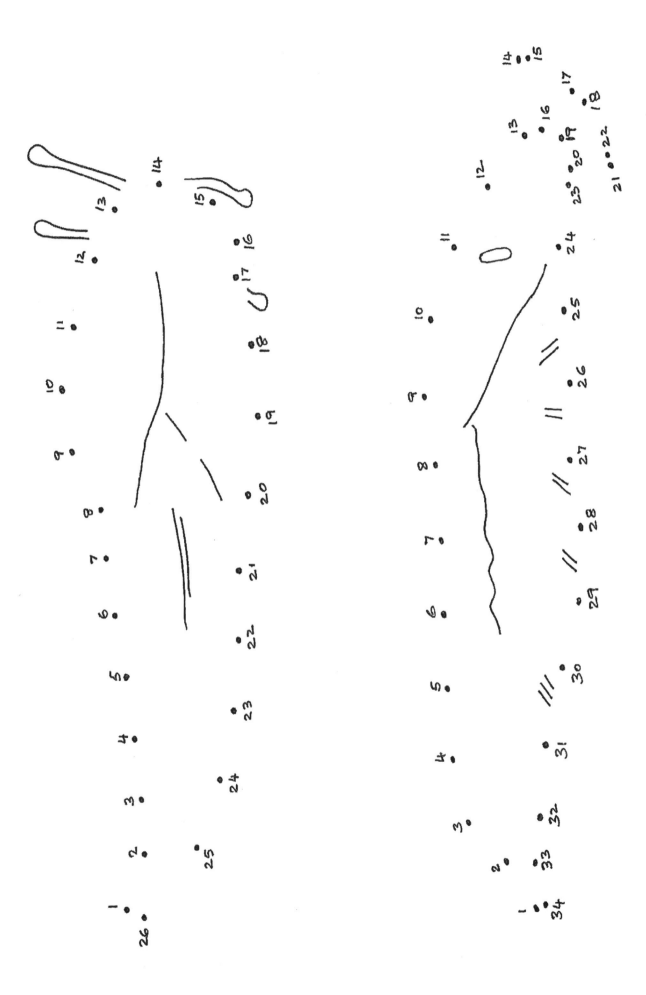

24

23 25
22 26
21 27

20 28

19   29
17 18   30

16 15   31
            32
13 14   33 34
12   35

1
8   2
11   36
7   3
10   37
6
9   4
8   5   38 39
7   40
45 50 55 60
6   41
44 46 49 51 54 56 61
42 47 48 52 53 57 58 59
5
4   43

3

28 29   2
27   30
26 31
17 18   19 25 32 39 40
16   24 33 38 41 1
15 20 34 42
14 21 37 36 43
13 22 35 44
12 11   45
10 46
9   47
8   48

5 6 4 50
4 7   51
3 52
2 53
1 54

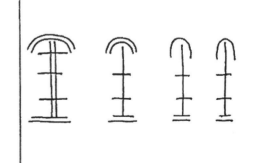

About The Author

Ruth Irwin lives in Wiltshire, with her family. Born in India, she grew up in the Himalayan foothills. Raised by loving Christian parents, and taught from an early age to love God and walk in His paths; she has found love, hope, peace, joy and comfort in Jesus Christ.

All of Ruth's books encourage the reader to find strength and comfort in the love and grace of God. They offer hope and encouragement, reaffirming to the reader that we are God's most treasured possessions.

She has more poetry books to enjoy, for example: "ISHI" and "REVEALED IN POETRY AND PROSE". Both of these delightful books have colour pictures included within their pages for the reader to enjoy alongside the poems. Ruth has also authored 'YOU, A SPIRITUAL BEING' and 'STAYING CONNECTED TO GOD' to bless and encourage, and share God's love.

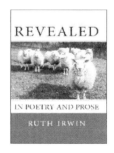   

All are available at AMAZON (as well as many other online bookstores)

Printed in Poland
by Amazon Fulfillment
Poland Sp. z o.o., Wrocław